Contents

INTRODUCTION

For starters, you will know exactly what's in your cat's food because you put it there yourself. Dry kibble tends to be loaded with carbohydrates and plant based proteins. Worse, it is often contaminated by bacteria, fungal mycotoxins and even vermin and their excretions. You want better nutrition for your cat.

Dry food also does not have a high enough moisture content for cats. Many people remember the mass pet food recalls in 2007 after many unfortunate animals experienced renal failure after eating contaminated food. If you cook your cat's food yourself, you will know exactly what she's eating and, almost as importantly, what she's not eating.

Now let's talk about costs. Will it be cheaper in the long run to cook your own cat food? That all depends. Are you using chicken or rabbit? Unless you own a warren, chicken will usually be cheaper. Are you getting your ingredients from Whole Foods, a typical grocery store or the farmer's market? Do you want to use supplements? Just how much does your cat eat? How much should your cat be eating? Do you prefer organic? Will you be willing to do your own prep work? All cats are different.

When considering how much your food bill will be for your cat, it's a good idea to weigh it against a possible vet bill. Cats that eat healthy

have better health and won't need to see a vet as

often. Plus, healthy cats are happy cats.

While cats are partial to routine, they do like

some variety in their diet. Making your cats

something new every few days is much better

than giving them the same food day after day,

only for them to turn their noses up at it out of

boredom.

HOMEMADE CAT FOOD

For starters, you will know exactly what's in your cat's food because you put it there yourself. Dry kibble tends to be loaded with carbohydrates and plant based proteins. Worse, it is often contaminated by bacteria, fungal mycotoxins and even vermin and their excretions. You want better nutrition for your cat.

Dry food also does not have a high enough moisture content for cats. Many people remember the mass pet food recalls in 2007 after many unfortunate animals experienced renal failure after eating contaminated food. If you cook your cat's food yourself, you will know exactly what she's eating and, almost as importantly, what she's not eating.

Now let's talk about costs. Will it be cheaper in the long run to cook your own cat food? That all depends. Are you using chicken or rabbit? Unless you own a warren, chicken will usually be cheaper. Are you getting your ingredients from Whole Foods, a typical grocery store or the farmer's market? Do you want to use supplements? Just how much does your cat eat? How much should your cat be eating? Do you prefer organic? Will you be willing to do your own prep work? All cats are different.

When considering how much your food bill will be for your cat, it's a good idea to weigh it against a possible vet bill. Cats that eat healthy

have better health and won't need to see a vet as

often. Plus, healthy cats are happy cats.

While cats are partial to routine, they do like

some variety in their diet. Making your cats

something new every few days is much better

than giving them the same food day after day,

only for them to turn their noses up at it out of

boredom.

Besides the pride you'll feel in creating tasty treats, there are numerous real benefits to homemade cat food.

- It's more natural. Cats are highly-evolved predators. A diet made entirely of commercial cat foods can meet their nutritional needs, but will not satisfy their carnivorous instincts as well as the best home recipes.
- It's healthier. Kitties have sharp, pointy teeth that were meant to slice and tear through raw meat. Processed foods don't provide the same oral health benefits.

There are countless health benefits to natural foods.

- It's easier to digest. As your little predator chomps and chews her way through your delicious meal, signals are sent to her stomach to prepare essential gastric acids to aid in digestion.

- It's more fun. Kitty will have a lot more fun eating the recipes we've prepared on this list – and you'll have a lot more fun watching her eat!

- It's easier to control. The fact is, by sourcing your ingredients and owning the process, you will have complete control over your cat's diet.

TYPES OF HOMEMADE CAT FOOD

CAT RAW DIET

Homemade cat food can be as time-consuming or as simple as you want it to be. You don't need to have endless free time or be a nutrition expert to prepare food for your cat. You can make cooked food, raw food, or semi-cooked food.

HOMEMADE RAW

This is the most popular type of homemade cat food. It requires minimal supplementation compared to cooked foods. That doesn't mean that raw food alone is an adequate diet. You'll still need to add supplements to ensure that the food is nutritionally complete.

While some express concerns about the potential bacteria content of raw meat, it's important to remember that your cat's stomach acid is about 10 times more concentrated than a human's. Cats have been eating dead animals for thousands of years. Bacteria is more a concern for you than it is for them.

HOMEMADE SEMI-COOKED

Semi-cooked food undergoes a brief baking process, which kills surface bacteria and renders the food safer than a purely raw product. It does, however, introduce some nutritional variables.

It's difficult to know exactly how much nutrient

value is destroyed during par-cooking.

HOMEMADE COOKED

Homemade cooked food is great for people

worried about pathogenic bacteria, parasites,

and other organisms that could make them or

their cats ill. However, it's more difficult to get a

complete and balanced homemade cooked diet

than a raw one.

HOW DO YOU KNOW YOUR HOMEMADE CAT FOOD IS NUTRITIONALLY COMPLETE AND HEALTHY?

Not all homemade cat food recipes are nutritionally complete, nor are they all balanced. When researchers from the University of California, Davis School of Veterinary Medicine analyzed 200 different homemade dog food recipes in cookbooks and online guides, the team found that 95% lacked at least one key nutrient. Only four of the recipes analyzed were nutritionally complete and balanced.

Our cats are genetically almost identical to African wildcats. Unlike dogs, their dietary needs have not evolved from their ancient roots. Indeed, cats have only been eating commercial human-made food for the last century. Prior to that, they ate what they always have—lizards, rodents, birds, and bugs.

After putting together 27 studies on the diet of free-roaming cats, the authors of an article published in the British Journal of Nutrition reached some conclusions about nature's dietary requirements.

They found that the macronutrient content of a feral cat's diet, with essentially no access to human food or garbage, was 52% crude protein, 46% crude fat, and only 2% calories from N-free extract, a term that refers to everything that's not fat, fiber, or protein.

WHAT YOU'LL NEED TO MAKE HOMEMADE CAT FOOD

MEAT GRINDER (OPTIONAL, BUT RECOMMENDED)

If you are cooking your cat's food, it is okay to feed them pre-ground meat with supplements mixed in. If you're feeding it raw, grind it yourself the day you prepare the food.

When most butchers grind meat, they know that the meat will be cooked before anyone eats it. This means that ground meat is held to a low sanitation standard compared to meat ground to eat raw.

Ideally, you'll use a powerful meat grinder to grind your meat with the bones intact. If you don't have a grinder strong enough to handle bones, you should either upgrade or use a grinder-free method.

MAKING HOMEMADE CAT FOOD WITHOUT A GRINDER

If you have a Vitamix or equally powerful blender or food processor, you may use it instead of a meat grinder. Other less powerful blenders won't be able to handle the bones, so don't risk it.

If you don't have a Vitamix or a grinder, you can make your cat food without bones.

Instead of taking the ultra-natural approach and grinding the meat and bones together, you can use boneless meat and a bone substitute like bone meal powder or eggshell powder. One route is to use a food processor or blender to grind the boneless meat and organs. While it will take more time, you can also mince the meat with a knife. Here's a guide to grinding meat by hand.

Whatever method you choose, I recommend leaving a few chunks of meat for your cat to chew and gnaw. This is good for their teeth and, I believe, emotionally nourishing for your cat.

CUTTING BOARD

When dealing with large quantities of raw meat, a large cutting board really makes life more comfortable. Regardless of size, your cutting board should be dishwasher-safe so that you can easily give it a thorough cleaning.

After using a small cutting board and constantly worrying about meat sliding onto the counter, I finally invested in this large board. It's transformed my attitude towards preparing

homemade cat food.

KITCHEN SCALE (OPTIONAL)

These allow you to measure out precise amounts

of meat and organs, ensuring that the recipe is

balanced. You'll be weighing large amounts of

meat, so be sure to get one that can handle at

least 10 lbs. If you don't have a kitchen scale and

aren't prepared to buy one now, you can ask

your butcher to measure specific amounts of

meat and organs.

Once you've gone through your checklist of preparation supplies, it's time to get your hands on some ingredients.

A cat's prey is approximately 83% meat, fat, skin, sinew, connective tissue, and heart, with 7% edible bone, 5% liver, and 5% other secreting organs. You'll need to include muscle meat, bones, organs, and supplements.

WHICH TYPE OF MEAT IS BEST?

To prevent your cat from developing food allergies, feed a rotational diet and don't become reliant on any one animal protein source.

Chicken is an economical, easy-to-find meat.

Chicken organs are easy to find in most grocery

stores, so there's no need to seek out a butcher

shop or go out of your way to find liver and other

organs.

Another nice thing about chicken and poultry, in

general, is that it has a high meat-to-bone ratio.

Bones are an essential part of a homemade diet,

but it's possible to give your cat too much,

resulting in constipation or over-mineralization.

The latter can lead to urinary crystals.

You can use either whole carcasses or parts of

the birds. If you choose to buy cuts of poultry,

feed about 75% dark meat and 25% white meat.

Dark meat has more appropriate fat levels, is more nutrient-dense, and contains more taurine, but white meat has methionine, which can help to prevent FLUTD.

TURKEY

Turkey thighs, breast meat, and organs are usually very appetizing to cats and can be a good alternative to chicken for poultry-loving felines. If you can't find turkey hearts or livers, you can substitute chicken parts.

What's great about rabbit is that it's a natural part of the feline diet. Some domesticated cats kill and eat wild rabbits half their size.

Rabbit is lean and is skinned prior to processing, so you'll want to add in additional animal fat from poultry or other animals. Remember, also, that rabbit has a higher bone-to-meat ratio than poultry, so you may want to remove some of the bones before preparing rabbit-based homemade cat food.

OTHER OPTIONS

You can feed your cat almost any type of meat that's convenient for you. Whenever feeding wild game, it's important to freeze the meat to kill parasites before preparing your cat's food.

MEATS TO AVOID

Don't feed your cat wild boar, pig, bear, or—if you can get it—walrus meat. These may transmit pseudorabies. Don't feed your cat squirrel, either, due to the potential for leptospirosis transmission.

Though it's scrumptious and makes a great snack, ocean fish is contaminated with heavy metals and toxins, making it an inappropriate choice for daily feeding. Cats who consume a raw diet comprised primarily of fish are at risk of thiamine deficiency.

ORGANS AND HEARTS

LIVER

Liver is jam-packed with nutrients. It's an excellent source of vitamin A and D, along with copper and zinc. Chicken liver is the most commonly available type, but you can get it from almost any other animal. It's important to note that beef liver has more copper than liver from other animals. If feeding your cat a beef-based diet, be sure to source liver from another species.

Hearts are muscle meat, but in contrast to other types of muscle meat, heart is rich in taurine. Cats cannot synthesize this amino acid, but it's essential for good health. Chicken hearts are the easiest types of heart to source, but they're not as taurine-dense as a mouse heart. For this reason, you can't rely on hearts alone as a source of taurine. It's important to add a taurine supplement.

RAW CAT FOOD OR COOKED?

To quote a popular meme, "Why not both?"
People who are against raw food are worried
about parasites and bacteria. People who are
against cooked food are concerned about the
loss of nutrients in their cats diet. In this case, it's
better to look at the positive benefits each side
has, use a little common sense and compromise.
Consider par-cooking, heating it just enough to
eliminate the surface bacteria.

Use the same food safety precautions you would
for preparing raw meat for human consumption.
Do not cross-contaminate by using cutting
boards and utensils used for raw meat on
vegetables, store the meat at 40 degrees

Fahrenheit or below and above all, wash your hands. Ground meat tends to have a lot of surface bacteria mixed in, but if you use your own grinder and keep it clean, it should be fine. (No pun intended.)

Keep in mind, your cat has different nutritional needs than yours. She can eat not only raw meat, but the organs that you might find disgusting. However, older pets being transitioned to homemade food diet and cats with sensitive or damaged gastrointestinal tracts might benefit more from a cooked food diet.

If you do cook meat for your cat, she might not only prefer it to be very rare, but it's more nutritionally sound for her. Rare meat still has those healthy enzymes while all surface bacteria

has been killed off, plus it's still nice and moist.

Avoid sausage meat and other manufactured

meat as they contain sulfite preservatives that

are not good for cats. In any case, consult a

veterinarian before feeding your cat anything out

of the ordinary for her.

The one place where raw versus cooked comes

down to one or the other is when bones are

involved. If your cat gnaws on bones, they should

be raw rather than cooked as cooked bones can

splinter and hurt your cat. Even then, supervise

your cat's gnawing and remember that more

than one or two a week in your cats diet can lead

to constipation.

THE ESSENTIAL NUTRIENTS NEEDED IN CATS' DIET:

ANIMAL PROTEIN

The cat is an obligate carnivore. Cats needs meat in their food to survive. Some cat foods will try to tout themselves as "high protein" only for it to be later revealed that the protein sources were soy, nuts, lentils or wheat gluten. This will not do. Cats can only digest protein from animal sources.

The domestic cat has the shortest digestive tract to body size ratio of any mammal. This makes it very hard for them to digest plant based protein.

ANIMAL FATS

You might want to cut down on fat but your cat doesn't! Cats needs easily digestible fats in their diet for energy. Specifically, cats need omega-6 fatty acids such as linolic and arachidonic acid. Fish oil, krill oil and flaxseed are all good sources of omega-3 fatty acids but you can also use poultry, beef and pork to get that healthy animal protein as well. If your cat has pancreatitis, you may want to feed her something lower in fat.

CALCIUM AND PHOSPHORUS

Calcium and phosphorus are necessary for strong bones and teeth and is needed in your cats diet.

Calcium is also needed to help blood clot and phosphorus boosts the reparation of cells. Phosphorus will help your cat metabolize protein and calcium helps those lightning quick muscles work. Small fishes like sardines and anchovies are calcium rich because their bones are tiny enough to be edible.

TAURINE

This is a crucial amino acid that your cat cannot create for herself and must get it from the food she eats. Natural sources are lamb, beef, eggs, shellfish, cold water fish, brewer's yeast and dark chicken meat. Boiling meat can destroy the taurine present. Cats that do not eat enough taurine have vision and heart problems along with a general failure to thrive.

It is available as a nutritional supplement. The powdered form may be easiest to cook with.

WATER

Cats don't usually drink as much water as they should. Their wild ancestors lived in dry climates and they got most of their needed moisture from prey. Because of this, a modern cat has little instinct to drink water. What's more, cats can be picky about what kind of water they drink. Feed your cats food that's good and moist to make sure she's staying hydrated.

Cats may like their food mixed in with a little meat based broth (preferably no salt added) to make it more succulent.

VITAMINS

Your cat needs her nutrition and would be better off getting them from food sources than supplements in their diet. Cats can't convert beta-carotene from plant sources into vitamin A, so it needs to come from an animal source such as halibut, liver and kidneys. Beef liver is also a good source of vitamin D as are tuna, mackerel and salmon in your cats diet.

To help your cat have a healthy coat, vitamin E can be found in eggs. The B vitamins are essential to a cat's well being and can be found in liver, brown rice, poultry, fish and red meat.

INGREDIENTS TO AVOID IN YOUR CATS DIET

This is no time to get experimental. You might like a little pep from onions and garlic, but your cat certainly will not. Onions and garlic are a big no-no to a cat's diet! Raw egg whites might have looked like they were good for Rocky Balboa, but they're not for your cat. While cats can safely eat many foods raw, eggs are a big exception.

Tomatoes, grapes and anything made with grapes should not be given to your cat in her diet. Chocolate is a big NO as is anything with caffeine. Adult cats can't process most dairy products. Keep the sherry in the cabinet. Your cat can't taste sweets and sugar isn't good for your cats health anyway.

HOMEMADE CAT FOOD COOKBOOK

CHICKEN CAT FOOD RECIPE

EQUIPMENT

Oven

- 1 cup Water (or more if your cat will eat it with more water)

- 2 Eggs. Use the yolk raw but lightly cook the white (soft boiling them works well) (optional - if your cat won't eat the food, try removing the eggs. Some cats just don't like them.)

- 5,000 - 10,000 IU Fish oil (5-10 capsules of the average 1,000 mg capsule) Fish oil is a good source of essential fatty acids. Do not use COD liver oil!

- 400 IU or (268 mg) Vitamin E (powdered E in capsules is the easiest to use)

- 50 mg Vitamin B-complex (capsules or tablets)

- 2,000 IU Taurine (use powdered - either in capsules or loose)

- 1 tsp Morton Lite salt with iodine

- 4 oz chicken livers per 3 lb of meat/bones/skin

- 2 1/3 tbsp tablespoons bone meal

- 3 lbs chicken thighs, with skin, bones removed (do not remove fat or skin - these are necessary ingredients for kitty health!)

INSTRUCTIONS

- Bake (at 350 degrees) the chicken/turkey thighs and liver leaving ~50% of the thigh meat raw. (The time needed varies depending on how thick the thighs are but is usually ~15 minutes, give or take.) The liver will be cooked more than the meat which is fine.

- Remove from the oven and put in cold water to stop the cooking process.

- Remove some of the raw meat from the bone for chunking (for the version in the picture, I used a grinder, if you use meat shears or a knife to "chunk" the meat - cutting it into small pieces about the size of a dime, it will look like the second picture). The bigger, the better. Keep in mind that raw meat is more tenacious (and better for teeth) than cooked meat. Make sure that you include the skin and all the fat!

- If using eggs, make sure you cook the whites (the yolks can be cooked or left raw). Break the egg into small pieces so that it incorporates into the rest of the ingredients.

- Mix together the meat/liver/skin, egg whites, and fat drippings in one large bowl. Placed mixture in the refrigerator while the supplements are mixed up.

- Combine the water, egg yolks (if you only cooked the white versus the whole egg), vitamin E, vitamin B-complex, taurine, salt, bone meal, and fish oil with a whisk. Note that it is helpful to put the fish oil capsules in warm water in advance of mixing up the supplement slurry. It takes about 15 minutes for them to dissolve and I use my hand to make sure that all of the oil is squeezed out of each capsule. Some people poke the fish oil capsules with a pin. It is ok to leave the capsules in the water. Most cats readily eat them but if your cat is not fond of fish, then you may want to remove them.

- Pour the supplement slurry into the meat/skin/liver/egg mixture. Mix very well.

- Portion into containers and freeze. Leave at least 3/4" of head space to allow for expansion.

- Ideally, the food should only be in the refrigerator (in a completely thawed state) for 48 - 72 hours so keep that in mind when choosing your container size. The average cat eats about 3.5-6 ounces per day.

CHICKEN AND GREENS

INGREDIENTS

- 3 lb Quartered Roasting Chicken

- 4 cup Water

- 1/2 teaspoon Salt

- 2 piece Celery stalks with leaves

- 1 cup Carrots, finely chopped

- 2 tablespoon Parsley flakes or 1/2 cup

  chopped fresh parsley

- 1/2 cup Barley, uncooked

- 1 tablespoon Lemon juice

- 3 teaspoon Brewer's yeast

- 5 ounce Thawed and drained chopped

  frozen spinach

- 1 cup Fresh green beans, chopped

INSTRUCTIONS

- Place chicken, salt, water and the celery

  leaves in a large stockpot or slow cooker.

  (Save the celery stalks.) Cover, bring to a

boil. Reduce heat and simmer for 1 to one and a half hours or until chicken is tender.

- Remove chicken and strain broth into a bowl. Chill broth in refrigerator until top is covered in fat. Skim fat.

- Remove fat, skin, and bones from chicken. Discard. Cut meat into bite sized pieces. Set aside.

- Return broth to pot. Add chopped celery with carrots, barley, brewer's yeast and lemon juice. Cover and simmer 20 minutes.

- Add chicken, spinach and green beans. Cook 15 more minutes until beans are tender. Cool and serve. It will keep refrigerated for one week or frozen for a month in an airtight container.

RAW CHICKEN CAT FOOD

INGREDIENTS

- 4.5 lbs chicken thighs, bone and skin included

- 14 oz chicken hearts (can be substituted with a meat based source with 4000mg taurine supplement)

- 7 oz chicken livers

- 2 cups water

- 4 whole eggs or yolks (if your cat likes them)

- 200 mg Vitamin B supplement

- 200 IU Vitamin E

- dash of light iodized salt (Use sparingly. Too much salt is not good for your cat.)

- 200 mg Taurine

INSTRUCTIONS

- Remove and discard roughly half of the skin and 20% of the bone.

- Dice and slice most of thighs into small bite-sized portions.

- Grind the rest of the thigh meat, bones, hearts, and liver. Stir until well blended.

- In large bowl, combine all vitamin supplements, eggs, and salt. Add 2 cups of water. Eggs should be well whisked.

- You will now have three main mixtures; sliced/sheared meat, ground meat/bone, and supplements beaten with eggs. Combine and mix all ingredients thoroughly.

- The leftovers must be stored in an airtight container that allows room for expansion as the food freezes. You can put a few days worth of the meal in the refrigerator and freeze the rest.

MACKEREL RECIPE

EQUIPMENT

food processor

INGREDIENTS

- 1 cup canned mackerel

- 1 tbsp sunflower seed oil

- 1 tbsp organic cooked brown rice

- 1-2 tbsp water or broth (chicken or beef)

INSTRUCTIONS

- Combine all ingredients in food processor.

- Puree until blended.

- It is best if served immediately but you can refrigerate the leftovers up to three days.

TROUT DINNER

EQUIPMENT

food processor

INGREDIENTS

- 1 cup trout, fully cooked

- 1 cooked egg yolk

- 1 tbsp fine chopped broccoli, steamed

- 2 tbsp sunflower oil

INSTRUCTIONS

- Combine all ingredients in food processor.

- Puree until blended and serve.

- As with mackerel dinner, leftovers can be stored in the refrigerator up to three days.

CHICKEN DINNER

EQUIPMENT

food processor

INGREDIENTS

- 1 cup broiled or baked chicken
- 1/4 cup mashed steamed broccoli
- 1/4 cup mashed steamed carrots
- Chicken broth, separated

INSTRUCTIONS

- Place ingredients in food processor with tablespoons of the chicken broth.
- Puree or crumble the ingredients until it resembles pate cat food. Gradually add broth until mixture is smooth but not soupy.

- Serve at room temperature.

DELUXE FISH BALLS RECIPE

EQUIPMENT

Oven

INGREDIENTS

- 1 Small can of oil packed tuna fish

- 2 tbsp bread crumbs

- 1 egg, well beaten

- 3 tbsp or 45 milliliters of grated cheese

INSTRUCTIONS

- Preheat oven to 350 degrees.

- Mash all ingredients together until a

  paste-like mixture forms.

- Shape into balls and place on greased baking tray.

- Bake for 20 minutes. Check frequently. When they are golden brown and firm, they are ready.

- Cool before serving.

CHICKEN AND TUNA DINNER

EQUIPMENT

food processor

INGREDIENTS

- 1/2 cup cooked chicken

- 1 can oil packed tuna

- 1 tbsp mashed cooked carrot

- Combine all ingredients in the food processor

- Puree until blended and serve.

- As with trout and mackerel dinners, you may refrigerate leftovers. Discard them after three days.

TUNA PATTIES

INGREDIENTS

- 1 can tuna, drained

- 1/2 cup cooked rice

- 1/4 cup liver, pureed

- 2-3 sprigs chopped parsley

- Mix all ingredients together with drained tuna

- Make six or seven balls. Form into patties.

- Serve and store leftovers in the refrigerator.

KITTY BREAKFAST

INGREDIENTS

- 1 tbsp dry milk, nonfat

- 3 medium sized eggs

- 3 tbsp cottage cheese

- 2 tbsp grated vegetables

- Mix milk powder and a small amount of water together.

- Add eggs. Beat until well blended.

- Pour the mixture into small non-stick frying pan. Cook over medium-low heat until done.

- Flip as you would a pancake and spread cottage cheese and vegetables over half of cooking surface. Fold as you would an omelet. Cool and cut into bite-sized pieces before serving.

RABBIT STEW

INGREDIENTS

- 1/2 lb Rabbit meat

- 1 tsp olive oil

- A dash of parsley, thyme, rosemary, and marjoram

- Unsalted vegetable stock

- 20 grams sweet potato, carrot, celery, and peas

INSTRUCTIONS

- Sautee rabbit in the olive oil

- Sprinkle with herbs and add vegetable stock, bringing to a boil.

- Reduce heat and cook through.

- Add chopped veggies and return to the

  oven for another 45 mins.

- Let cool to room temperature and serve.

- You may opt to put it through your food

  processor to "pre-chew" it for your cat.

  This might aid in the digestion process

  and help her consume the veggies.

  (optional)

- Store leftovers in an airtight container for

  up to 3 days in the fridge, or freeze

CAT SALAD

Many cats like greens, but indoor cats usually

don't have access to the grass they crave. This

special treat should satisfy your cat's craving for
something green.

INGREDIENTS

- 1/4 cup grated zucchini

- 1/2 cup chopped alfalfa sprouts

- 1/8 cup chicken or fish stock

- 1/8 teaspoon of minced catnip for garnish

DIRECTIONS

- Combine the first three ingredients in a
  bowl and toss.

- Serve sprinkled with the minced catnip on
  top.

- Leftovers can be stored in a covered
  container in a refrigerator for up to three
  days.

EGGS FOR BREAKFAST

Eggs with cottage cheese should be your cat's first meal of the day. Here is how you can make a nutritious breakfast for your cat rich with eggs and cottage cheese.

INGREDIENTS

- 3 medium eggs
- 2 tablespoons of veggies of your cat's choice (grated)
- 1 tablespoon non-fat dry milk
- 3 tablespoons cottage cheese

DIRECTIONS

- In a medium to large size bowl, take the milk powder, add water to it, and mix it well. Make sure that there are no lumps in it.

- Break and add the 3 medium eggs into the mixture and beat well.

- Take a frying pan and preheat it on a medium to high flame. Pour the entire mixture and cook it, as you would do with while making pancakes.

- Flip it, add the cut veggies and grated cottage cheese on the half-cooked side and allow it to cook well.

- Once it is cooked, fold it in half like an omelette and cut into bite-size pieces. Serve it warm in your cat's favourite bowl.

CHICKEN STEW

This meal is super easy to cook and can be used both for lunch as well as dinner.

INGREDIENTS

- 2 cups of brown rice
- 8 carrots (scrubbed but not peeled)
- Boneless chicken
- ¼ cup of green peas
- A handful of green beans

DIRECTIONS

- Wash the chicken in and out and keep it in a large stew pot and cover it with water till the brim.

- Take the veggies and cut them into small

  pieces and add them to the pot.

- Add the 2 cups of brown rice.

- Cook till the chicken becomes soft and the

  veggies are soft enough to consume.

- Take the entire stew and pour it into a

  large blender. Blend it.

- Let the mixture cool down a bit and serve

  in your pet's favourite bowl whenever he

  feels a bit hungry.

THE CLASSIC CHICKEN

The classic chicken diet is a pet-parent favourite

across the world.

INGREDIENTS

- 1/2 pound chicken breast (boneless and cooked)

- 1/8 teaspoon salt substitute

- 1/2 large egg (hard-boiled, split it lengthwise)

- 2 tablespoons of olive oil

DIRECTIONS

- Take all the ingredients in a microwave-safe bowl and mix them well.

- Heat it up in the microwave oven before serving it to your cat.

CHICKEN AND RICE

Chicken and rice is a great combination for all pets.

INGREDIENTS

- 1/3 pound chicken breast (boneless and cooked)
- 1/3 cup long-grain rice (cooked)
- 1 egg (hard boiled and mashed)
- 2 teaspoons of olive oil
- 1/8 teaspoon salt substitute
- 1 multiple vitamin-mineral tablet (crushed)

DIRECTIONS

- Take all the ingredients in a large bowl.

- Mix the entire list of ingredients using both your hands and serve meal size portions in your pet's favourite bowl.

FISH

Cats love to eat fish, so make it a part of your cat's diet – he will thank you for that.

INGREDIENTS

- Depending on your cat's age choose a small, medium or large fish with preferably fewer bones.

- 1 egg (hard-boiled and chopped)

- 1 multiple vitamin-mineral tablet

- 2 bone meal tablets (crushed, 10-grain or

  equivalent)

- Take a large bowl and add all the

  ingredients in it except the fish.

- Boil the fish for 10 to 20 minutes so that

  its flesh becomes soft and remove the

  bones.

- Add the fish meat to the bowl and mix all

  the ingredients properly.

- Heat it in a microwave and serve medium

  hot.

MACKEREL STARTER

This mackerel recipe is a favourite among cats and it is the perfect food you can make for your cat at home.

INGREDIENTS

- 1 cup cooked or canned mackerel

- 1 tablespoon sunflower oil

- 1 tablespoon of cooked brown rice

- 2 tablespoons of chicken broth

DIRECTIONS

- Mix all the ingredients in a blender and blend well.

- Serve immediately. You can store this in the fridge for three days.

SARDINE TREAT

Here's another fish meal that your cat will love.

INGREDIENTS

- Sardines (1 canned or 3 to 4 fresh ones)

- 2 tbsp of grated carrots

- 1/3 cup cooked oatmeal

DIRECTIONS

- Mix all the ingredients in a bowl and

  serve.

- You can refrigerate the leftovers and use

  it for 3 days.

DIABETES SPECIAL

Some pets have diabetes. They might develop it in the late stages of their lives or may even show symptoms from the very beginning. If your pet cat has diabetes, here's a cat food recipe for senior cats with diabetes.

INGREDIENTS

- 1/2 cup grains (brown rice or oatmeal, cooked)
- 1/2 cup organic chicken (raw, ground)
- 1/4 cup raw carrots or cooked green beans
- 1/2 cup chicken liver (raw)
- vegetable broth to moisten

- Take a large bowl and pour all the ingredients into it. Mix all the ingredients to the desired consistency.

- Warm up the meal before serving and serve in small bite-sized pieces for easy digestion.

- This meal is specially designed for cats with diabetes and its main aim is to strengthen the pancreas, reduce insulin needs and reduce scarring.

CONCLUSION

Cooking food for your cat is a bit of an adventure, but both you and your cat will enjoy the rewards!

Talk with your veterinarian before making any drastic changes to your cat's diet. Make sure your cat eats only what's good for her and gets all the vitamins and minerals she needs.

9 798685 890146